**W9-AOK-183**

Seven Natural Wonders of
CENTRAL *and*
SOUTH AMERICA

Michael Woods and Mary B. Woods

TWENTY-FIRST CENTURY BOOKS

Minneapolis

To Jacqueline Rosen and Lynette Curran

Copyright © 2009 by Michael Woods and Mary B. Woods

All rights reserved. International copyright secured. No part of this book may be reproduced, stored in a retrieval system, or transmitted in any form or by any means—electronic, mechanical, photocopying, recording, or otherwise—without the prior written permission of Lerner Publishing Group, Inc., except for the inclusion of brief quotations in an acknowledged review.

Twenty-First Century Books
A division of Lerner Publishing Group, Inc.
241 First Avenue North
Minneapolis, MN 55401 U.S.A.

Website address: www.lernerbooks.com

Library of Congress Cataloging-in-Publication Data

Woods, Michael, 1946–
    Seven natural wonders of Central and South America / by Michael Woods and Mary B. Woods.
      p. cm. — (Seven wonders)
    Includes bibliographical references and index.
    ISBN 978–0–8225–9070–5 (lib. bdg. : alk. paper)
    1. Landforms—Central America—Juvenile literature. 2. Landforms—South America—Juvenile literature. 3. Rivers—Central America—Juvenile literature. 4. Rivers—South America—Juvenile literature. I. Woods, Mary B. (Mary Boyle), 1946– II. Title.
    GB429.W66 2009
    508.8–dc22   2008027203

Manufactured in the United States of America
1 2 3 4 5 6 – DP – 14 13 12 11 10 09

Contents

INTRODUCTION

$\mathcal{P}$EOPLE LOVE TO MAKE LISTS OF THE BIGGEST AND THE BEST. ALMOST TWENTY-FIVE HUNDRED YEARS AGO, A GREEK WRITER NAMED HERODOTUS MADE A LIST OF THE MOST AWESOME THINGS EVER BUILT BY PEOPLE. THE LIST INCLUDED BUILDINGS, STATUES, AND OTHER OBJECTS THAT WERE LARGE, WONDROUS, AND IMPRESSIVE. LATER, OTHER WRITERS ADDED NEW ITEMS TO THE LIST. WRITERS EVENTUALLY AGREED ON A FINAL LIST. IT WAS CALLED THE SEVEN WONDERS OF THE ANCIENT WORLD.

The list became so famous that people began imitating it. They made other lists of wonders. They listed Seven Wonders of the Modern World and Seven Wonders of the Middle Ages. People even made lists of undersea wonders.

People also made lists of natural wonders. Natural wonders are extraordinary things created by nature, without help from people. Earth is full of natural wonders, so it has been hard for people to choose the absolute best. Over the years, different people have made different lists of the Seven Wonders of the Natural World.

This book explores seven natural wonders from Central and South America. Like Earth as a whole, Central and South America have far more than seven natural wonders. But even if people can never agree on which ones are the greatest, these seven choices are sure to amaze you.

WONDERFUL PLACES

This book explores seven wonders of two areas of the world—Central and South America. Central America is the narrow strip of land between North America and South America. It includes the countries of Belize, Guatemala, El Salvador, Honduras, Nicaragua, Costa Rica, and Panama. About 41 million people call Central America home.

Almost 400 million people live in South America. It is the fourth-largest of Earth's seven continents. (Asia, Africa, and North America are bigger.) South America includes the countries of Argentina, Bolivia, Brazil, Chile, Colombia, Ecuador, Paraguay, Peru, Uruguay, Venezuela, Guyana, and Suriname. South America also includes French Guiana, which is a part of France. Several islands in the Pacific Ocean are also part of South America. They include Easter Island and the Galápagos Islands. Easter Island belongs to Chile, and the Galápagos Islands belong to Ecuador.

WONDERFUL ADVENTURE

This book will take you on a tour of some of Central and South America's natural wonders. The first stop on the tour is Angel Falls *(left)*, the world's highest waterfall. It plunges thousands of feet from the top of a mountain. Another stop on the tour is the Atacama Desert. At its center lies the driest desert land on Earth. We will also visit islands populated by very unusual creatures, including a vampire bird. These animals have helped change the science of biology. And don't miss the visit to an enchanted forest. In that forest, the plants wring water out of the clouds. Other fascinating places are waiting in between these visits. Read on to begin your adventure.

1 Angel Falls

Angel Falls pours over a cliff in Venezuela.

THE WORLD'S TALLEST WATERFALL IS IN VENEZUELA, A COUNTRY IN SOUTH AMERICA. ANGEL FALLS IS ONE OF THE MOST AWESOME NATURAL FORMATIONS ON EARTH. WHEN THE WIND BLOWS JUST RIGHT, THIS TALL STREAM OF WATER SWIRLS, BENDS, AND SWAYS THROUGH THE AIR. SUNLIGHT SHINES ON AIR THAT IS WET FROM THE WATERFALL'S SPRAY. THE SUNLIGHT OFTEN CREATES DOUBLE RAINBOWS. BEAUTIFUL BANDS OF RED, ORANGE, YELLOW, GREEN, BLUE, AND VIOLET ARCH OVER THE RUSHING WATER.

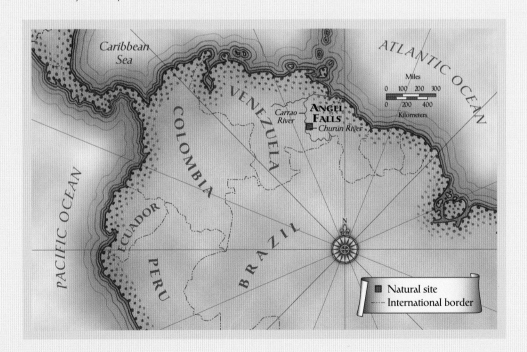

"We saw it [the mountain] afar off, and it appeared like a white church tower of an exceeding height. There falleth over it a mighty river . . . [that] falleth to the ground with a terrible roar and clamor, as if a thousand great bells were knocked one against another. I think there is not in the world so strange an overfall [waterfall]."

—Sir Walter Raleigh, an English explorer who visited Venezuela in the 1580s

When a river or stream tumbles over a cliff, the moving water drops suddenly. That sudden drop produces a waterfall. A branch of the Churún River creates Angel Falls as it plunges off a cliff at the edge of a mountaintop. The mountain does not have a rounded peak like most mountains. Instead, it is flat on top. The name of this mountain is Auyantepui. Other flat-topped mountains surround it. In Spanish they are called *tepuis*.

The waterfall is in the southeastern part of Venezuela. It is 3,212 feet (979 meters) high. That's more than eighteen times the height of Niagara Falls, in North America. Angel Falls plunges into a pool of water at its base. The pool connects to a branch of the Carrao River. The river flows through the surrounding canyon, past Auyantepui.

TERROR ON THE TEPUIS

The waterfall is a heavenly sight. But that is not why it is called Angel Falls. The story behind the name is an adventure tale. It is about a hunger for gold and riches. And it is also about courage.

In 1921 J. R. McCracken decided to go to Venezuela. McCracken was a gold prospector from Alaska. He spent his time searching for gold. McCracken heard about a mountaintop in Venezuela where gold nuggets lay on the ground like seashells scattered on a beach. So he went to South America. After McCracken arrived, he hired a U.S. pilot named James Angel to meet him in Venezuela. Angel agreed to fly McCracken to the mountain.

The two men flew over flat-topped mountains along the border between Venezuela and Brazil. Angel did not know exactly where he was because

Boaters ride up the Churún River toward Angel Falls. A tepui, a distincive feature of the Venezuelan countryside, looms in the distance. While on a search to find gold on the top of a tepui, pilot James Angel discovered a waterfall plunging over the side of Auyantepui.

McCracken refused to give him a map of the area. He told Angel to land on one of the tepuis. McCracken collected 75 pounds (34 kilograms) of gold nuggets. When McCracken left Venezuela, he kept the mountain's location a secret. Angel spent the rest of his life searching for that flat-topped mountain and its treasure.

In 1935 Angel went on an expedition to the tepuis in southeastern Venezuela. He was flying his airplane near Auyantepui, when he saw an amazing sight. A waterfall spilled over the top of the flat-topped mountain. The waterfall was so high that it seemed to be pouring directly out of the sky. Angel did not stay to admire the waterfall. He continued searching for gold.

"I saw a waterfall that almost made me lose control of the plane. The cascade came from the sky."

—*pilot James Angel, 1935*

Above: *Angel's plane,* El Río Caroní, *is photographed atop Auyantepui, where it remained until 1970.* Left: *In a later expedition, Angel (left) returned to Angel Falls with his wife, Marie (center),* and Carlos Herrera *(right), a photographer and mapmaker.*

Two years later, Angel returned to Venezuela from the United States. He brought his wife and two gold prospectors along with him. This time Angel decided to land on Auyantepui to look for gold. There was plenty of room to land because Auyantepui was the largest flat-topped mountain in the region. Its top covered an area of 270 square miles (700 square kilometers).

Angel's decision created a nightmare. His plane got stuck in mud on top of the mountain. Angel, his wife, and the two gold prospectors were stranded in the wilderness. They spent the next eleven days struggling through the jungle to reach the nearest village. Stories about their adventure spread

ANGEL'S *Wings*

After his escape from the Venezuelan jungle in 1937, Jimmy Angel became famous, especially in Venezuela. His airplane remained on top of Auyantepui until 1970. Then the government sent a helicopter to fly the plane out. It was put on display outside an airport terminal in Ciudad Bolívar.

around the world. Auyantepui and its waterfall became famous too. The government of Argentina named Angel Falls in honor of Jimmy Angel.

Stories about the waterfall and the rugged jungle landscape lured other explorers to the area. Their photos and adventures created more interest among people in the outside world. No one was sure about the height of Angel Falls, however. Then, in 1949, a U.S. journalist named Ruth Robertson led an expedition to Angel Falls. She and other members of the expedition measured its height. They discovered that Angel Falls was the world's highest waterfall.

Ruth Robertson (below left) *and the members of her expedition made the trip to Angel Falls in 1949 with the help of local guides. She was the first person to measure the height of the falls.*

Angel Falls as seen from the foot of the tepui

Ever *Wonder?*

How high is Angel Falls compared to other waterfalls? At 3,212 feet (979 m), Angel Falls is slightly higher than the Tugela Falls in Natal National Park in the country of South Africa. Water from the Tugela River tumbles 3,110 feet (948 m) over a cliff in that park. The Utigord Falls in Norway is the world's third highest falls at 2,625 feet (800 m). Several other waterfalls are more than 2,000 feet (610 m) high, including Yosemite Falls in Yosemite National Park in California. Niagara Falls may be the most famous waterfall in North America, but it is less than 200 feet (61m) high.

These falls are in Canaima National Park, which is home to the local Pemón Indians. The Venezuelan government established the 7.4-million-acre (3 million hectare) park in 1962.

DEVIL'S MOUNTAIN

The Pemón people have lived near Angel Falls for centuries. They knew about the falls long before Jimmy Angel arrived. They named the mountain Auyantepui, which means "Devil's Mountain" in English.

Auyantepui frightened the Pemón They believed evil spirits lived on this tepui. Over thousands of years, rain had worn away some of the soft sandstone on the mountain. This process of erosion had carved the stone into scary shapes.

A PREHISTORIC LANDSCAPE

The landscape surrounding Auyantepui looks prehistoric. There are more than one hundred flat-topped mountains in the region. These tepuis are the oldest rock formations visible on Earth's surface. They were formed more than a billion years ago. The steep sides of the mountains tower more than 3,280 feet (1,000 m) above the jungle. Some tepuis are blanketed by thick clouds most of the year.

The tepui tops have been isolated from the surrounding jungle for millions of years. They are almost like islands in a sea. As a result, they have unique forms of life. On the tepuis of Venezuela, some plants eat insects. Grasshoppers the size of lobsters live here. So do

"Spurting from a cliff more than half a mile [0.8 km] high in the jungle vastness of eastern Venezuela is Angel Falls, world's highest waterfall . . . more than twice the height of the Empire State Building."

—*journalist Ruth Robertson, 1949*

A tepui rises far above the surrounding Venezuelan landscape. These unusual mountains are Earth's oldest exposed rock formations. Each contains its own unique ecosystem.

prehistoric black frogs. Ancestors of these frogs crawled around the tepuis before the age of dinosaurs.

Angel Falls and most of the tepuis are in Venezuela's Canaima National Park. The government protects plant and animal life in this enormous area, which is larger than the state of Maryland. In 1994 the United Nations Educational, Scientific, and Cultural Organization (UNESCO) named the park a World Heritage Site in honor of its unique geological and other features. World Heritage Sites are places of great importance to all humanity. UNESCO tries to protect and preserve these sites for future generations. Because the area is so wild and isolated, visiting is difficult. Tourists usually hire a small airplane to fly over Angel Falls.

THE LOST *World*

The unusual region surrounding Angel Falls became famous in the early twentieth century. Several books contributed to the region's fame, even before the world learned about the waterfall. The most popular was *The Lost World* by Sir Arthur Conan Doyle. *The Lost World* was science fiction. It described an imaginary land inhabited by dinosaurs and prehistoric plants. Doyle had read stories that explorers wrote about the real world of the tepuis. Those stories inspired *The Lost World*. Doyle's book title stuck. People sometimes call this part of Venezuela the Lost World region.

A thrill-seeking BASE jumper leaps from the top of Angel Falls. BASE stands for Building, Antenna, Span, Earth—four types of fixed objects from which people jump. No doubt about it, Angel Falls has attracted its share of adventurers, naturalists, and daredevils.

2 Amazon River

The Amazon River snakes through the dense rain forest in Brazil.

*T*HE MIGHTY AMAZON RIVER FLOWS THROUGH THE NORTHERN PART OF SOUTH AMERICA. IT BEGINS AMONG THE TOWERING PEAKS OF THE ANDES MOUNTAINS IN PERU. THEN IT FLOWS NORTHEAST AND RUNS ACROSS BRAZIL. THE RIVER EMPTIES INTO THE ATLANTIC OCEAN NEAR THE EQUATOR.

The Amazon travels about 4,000 miles (6,437 km) from its source in the Andes to its mouth in the Atlantic Ocean. If it flowed across the United States, it could run from New York City to Los Angeles, California, and halfway back to New York again.

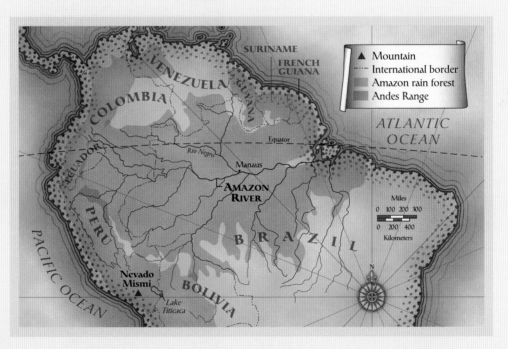

Experts disagree about the exact length of the Amazon River. As a result, they also disagree about whether the Amazon is the longest or second-longest river on Earth. Measuring rivers can be difficult. To determine a river's exact length, scientists try to find its source—where the river begins. The source may be an underground spring. Or it may be snow melting into a remote mountainside stream. To measure the river, the experts must decide exactly where the underground spring starts flowing aboveground. Or they must find the place where the melting snow starts gathering into a channel. Over the years, explorers from countries around the world have searched for the true source of the Amazon.

Many scientists believe the source of the Amazon River is in northern Peru. And they say the Nile River, in North Africa, is longer. The Nile is 4,135 miles (6,655 km) long.

In 2000, however, an expedition organized by the National Geographic Society traveled to southern Peru to find the river's source. The team announced that the source of this mighty river begins as a trickle of melting snow. They said the river's source is on a slope of a mountain called Nevado Mismi, in southern Peru. In 2007 Brazilian scientists traveled to Nevado Mismi. They agreed that the Amazon begins its journey on this mountain. The Brazilians determined that the Amazon is 4,225 miles (6,800 km) long. If they are correct, then the Amazon is the world's longest river.

EVER *Wonder?*

How did the Amazon River get its name? According to most historians, a Spanish explorer gave the river its name. In 1541 Francisco de Orellana *(below)* **was exploring the Amazon River. He later claimed he was attacked by a tribe of the local Tapuyas Indians. In that tribe, women fought alongside the men. The women warriors reminded de Orellana of the Amazons. They were female warriors in ancient Greek legends.**

There is another theory about the river's name. The Spanish name for the river, Amazona, might have come from a local word, *amassona.* **It means "boat destroyer." The Amazon's strong current threatened to sink the boats of the early Spanish explorers.**

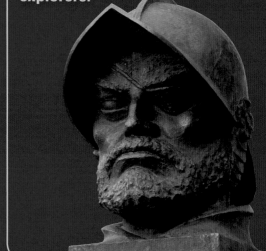

Oceangoing vessels ply the Amazon River near the inland city of Manaus, Brazil. There another river, Río Negro, joins the Amazon. Río Negro's black water is caused by decomposing rain forest plants. The muddy Amazon contains sediment from the eroding Andes Mountains.

BIG WATER

Eveyone agrees on one important fact: the Amazon carries more water than any other river in the world. The length, width, and depth of a river determine how much water it contains. The Amazon's average depth in the rainy season is 131 feet (40 m). (In regions of the central part of the river, the rainy season runs from December to May.) The river is so deep that large oceangoing ships can travel about 2,000 miles (3,219 km) inland from its mouth. Boats cannot go farther inland because the water is too shallow.

"The mightiest river in the world is the Amazon. It runs from west to east, from the sunset to the sunrise, from the Andes to the Atlantic. . . . [Its] gigantic river basin is filled with an immense forest, the largest in the world, with which no other forest can be compared save those of western Africa and Malaysia. We were within the southern boundary of this great equatorial forest."

—U.S. president Theodore Roosevelt, 1914

This satellite image of the mouth of the Amazon River shows the brownish silty water of the river entering the Atlantic Ocean.

Every second, the Amazon releases about 50 million gallons (189 million liters) of water into the Atlantic Ocean. During the rainy season, the river releases twice as much water. This enormous quantity of water creates a strong current of river water, which rushes into the ocean. The river water is freshwater. Unlike ocean water, it is not salty.

The Amazon's current of freshwater flows for about 125 miles (201 km) from the coast of Brazil out to sea. Then the water finally mixes with the Atlantic's salt water. Centuries ago, that current of freshwater told sailors that they were near Brazil long before they saw any land. Sailors felt the Amazon's current pushing against their ships. While still far out to sea, they dunked buckets into the current and enjoyed a drink of freshwater.

DRAINPIPE FOR THE RAIN FOREST

The Amazon is enormous because water from the entire northern half of South America flows into it. More than eleven hundred different rivers and streams drain into the Amazon. Seventeen of those rivers are more than 1,000 miles (1,609 km) long. Those rivers create the largest river system in the world. Almost 20 percent of Earth's freshwater is in the Amazon River system.

A gigantic tropical rain forest surrounds the Amazon River. It is the largest one on Earth. The Amazon rain forest is almost the size of the entire United States. It covers about 40 percent of South America. The Amazon rain forest is the wettest region on Earth. More than 80 inches (203 centimeters) of rain fall in the forest in an average year. That is almost twice the amount of rain that falls on New York City each year. Most of the water eventually collects in the Amazon River and flows down its mighty path.

People have lived in the rain forest for thousands of years. They have used the Amazon River as a highway for traveling from place to place. The river

Below left: *Brazilians in dugout canoes paddle on the Amazon.* Below right: *Rain forest plants crowd the riverbanks of the Amazon. The entire drainage area for the Amazon River and its tributaries contains some of the richest tropical rain forest on Earth.*

A three-toed sloth (below) *hangs in a rain forest tree. The Amazon rain forest is home to an immense number of species of plants and animals.*

has provided food as well as transportation. About two thousand species, or kinds, of fish swim in its waters. The forest is a treasure chest of biodiversity (different kinds of plants and animals). The Amazon has the largest collection of plants and animals in the world. More than one-third of all species of living things on Earth make their home in the Amazon. About 2.5 million species of insects crawl or fly in the lush rain forest. More than one hundred thousand kinds of plants grow there, such as lilies and brazil nut trees. Thousands of species of animals live among the trees and dense growth. These include jaguars, howler monkeys, and scarlet macaws, which are in the parrot family.

EXTREME *Creatures*

The mighty Amazon is full of life. One of the thousands of fish that swim in its waters is the piranha *(below)*. The piranha is the world's most ferocious fish. With their huge jaws and razor-sharp teeth, a school of piranha can devour a water ox within minutes.

Giant catfish live in the river too. In the United States, these creepy-looking fish, with big flat heads and "whiskers," may grow 5 feet (1.5 m) long and weigh 60 pounds (27 kg). In the Amazon, catfish may be the size of a large man, reaching a length of 6 feet (2 m) and a weight of 200 pounds (91 kg).

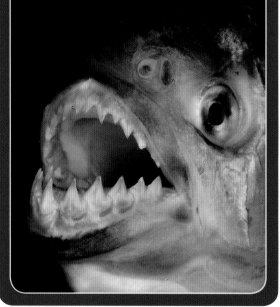

Above: *Giant river otters, which live in the rivers and streams of the Amazon rain forest, can grow to be 6 feet (1.8 m) long. They have become an endangered species.* Below left: *An emerald tree boa hangs from a branch. It spends its entire life in the trees.* Below right: *A saki monkey of the Amazon rain forest*

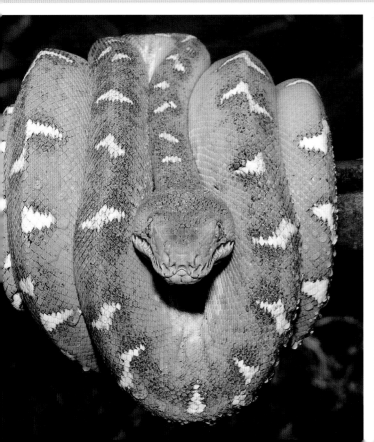

A Shrinking Rain Forest

People have been clearing land around the Amazon River since the 1600s. That is when the first Spanish settlers began raising cattle in the region. They cut down or burned areas of the rain forest. Then they planted grass so their cattle could graze. They also planted food crops. This process of destroying a rain forest is called deforestation.

As the years passed, loggers—the workers who cut down trees—cleared larger and larger

Brazilian plantation farmers cut down millions of acres of rain forest yearly to plant soybeans. In 2008 scientists worried that future rain forest land could be cut down for oil palm plantations. This has happened in rain forests in Asia.

Eating from the *Rain Forest*

Many of our favorite foods began as wild plants in the Amazon rain forest. These foods include oranges, lemons, pineapples, and bananas. The rain forest has also provided us with coconuts, peanuts, cashews, corn, rice, tomatoes, and even chocolate. The flavor of cola soft drinks comes from another Amazon native, the kola nut.

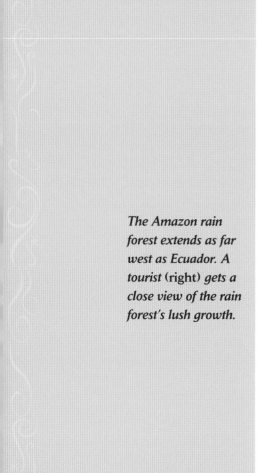

The Amazon rain forest extends as far west as Ecuador. A tourist (right) gets a close view of the rain forest's lush growth.

areas of forest. By the 1990s, the loggers were clearing about 7,700 square miles (19,943 sq. km) of rain forest each year. That's an area larger than the state of Connecticut. In addition, scientists have discovered that large amounts of oil and gas lie under the ground in untouched areas of the forest. Oil companies will clear trees to make roads and to bring in equipment as they search for places to drill.

The rate of deforestation in the Amazon rain forest slowed down in the early 2000s. But the rate is increasing again. If that trend continues, some scientists worry that much of the rain forest could disappear during the twenty-first century. Animals and plants that depend on the forest for a home and for food could become rare or extinct. They may no longer exist on Earth.

3 Atacama Desert

The landscape of the Atacama Desert in Chile is dry and deserted. In most parts of this desert, no plants grow and no animals live.

*V*ISITORS FROM ANOTHER PLANET MIGHT GET THE WRONG IDEA IF THEIR SPACECRAFT LANDS IN THE ATACAMA DESERT IN SOUTH AMERICA. THOSE EXTRATERRESTRIALS MIGHT DECIDE THAT NO LIFE EXISTS ON EARTH. MANY CREATURES THAT LIVE IN OTHER DRY PLACES CANNOT SURVIVE IN THIS DESERT. AMONG THEM ARE ANTS, SCORPIONS, SNAKES, AND BIRDS. IN SOME PARTS OF THE ATACAMA DESERT, THERE IS NO RECORD OF A SINGLE DROP OF RAIN *EVER* HAVING FALLEN. AT ITS VERY CENTER, THE ATACAMA IS THE DRIEST DESERT LAND ON EARTH.

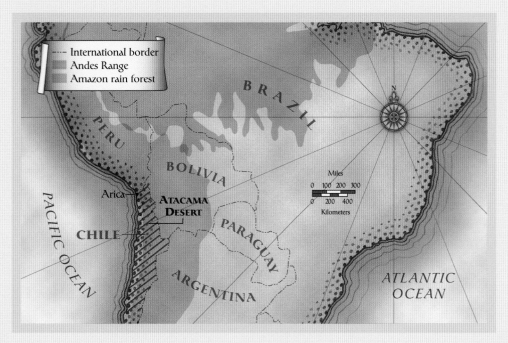

- - - International border
Andes Range
Amazon rain forest

BRAZIL

PERU

BOLIVIA

Arica

ATACAMA DESERT

CHILE

PACIFIC OCEAN

PARAGUAY

ARGENTINA

Miles
0 100 200 300
0   200   400
Kilometers

ATLANTIC OCEAN

The barren Atacama Desert is one of the driest places on Earth. The Andes rise in the distance.

The Atacama Desert is a strip of land that extends for 600 miles (965 km) through northern Chile. It is never more than 100 miles (160 km) wide. The desert begins on a plain near the Pacific Ocean. It rises onto a high plateau (flat land) and swings eastward into the Andes Mountains. In the Andes, the desert rises to an altitude of 22,590 feet (6,885 m) above sea level.

EXTREME DESERT

Deserts are not unusual. They cover more than 20 percent of Earth's surface. A desert is often defined as a place that receives less than an average of 10 inches (25 cm) of rain or snow per year.

The Atacama, however, is an extreme desert. In northern Chile, rainfall averages just 0.04 inch (1 millimeter) per year. That is only 1 percent of the rain that falls in most of the Sahara in Africa. Scientists have found that between 1570 and 1971, no rain fell in some parts of the Atacama. Scientific studies also came to surprising conclusions about some ancient riverbeds in the Atacama. Although rivers once flowed there, some of the riverbeds have been dry for at least 120,000 years.

"Towards Atacama, near the deserted coast, you see a land without men, where there is not a bird, not a beast, nor a tree, nor any vegetation."
—*Alonso de Ercilla, a Spanish poet who participated in the conquest of Chile in the 1500s*

The Atacama Desert has huge salt basins. Millions of years ago, the desert had a wetter climate. At that time, the salt basins were lakes filled with water. As the area grew hotter and drier, the water in the lakes evaporated (dried up). But the salts that were in the water remained in the dry basins. Water seeping up from deep below the ground also evaporated, adding to the salt deposits.

Salt gradually filled the dried-up lake basins to great depths. One of the salt basins has salt deposits more than 1,300 feet (396 m) thick. This salt basin covers an area of 1,160 square miles (3,004 sq. km).

This salt basin formed in the Atacama Desert when an ancient lake dried up, leaving behind salt.

Rain Shadow Desert

The Atacama is a rain shadow desert. It is a special kind of desert that forms on one side of a high mountain range. The mountains cast a shadow of dry weather behind them. They block masses of moist air that move across the land. When they reach the mountains, the moist air masses can move in only one direction: up and over the mountain. The air masses rise higher into the atmosphere, where the temperature is cooler. Cool air cannot hold as much moisture as warm air. So the moving air masses drop their moisture as rain or snow as they climb up the face of the mountain range. By the time air masses have passed over the mountain range to the other side, they are bone dry. There is no moisture to fall on the other side of the mountains. The result is a desert.

The Atacama Desert exists because the Andes Mountains cast a rain shadow. The Andes are east of the desert. They block the movement of moist air from the Amazon rain forest. In addition, weather patterns in the area prevent moist air from the Pacific Ocean from reaching the desert.

The dry mountains in the Atacama give way to the snowcapped peaks of the Andes in the distance.

DESERT
Scratch Pad

For almost one thousand years, the Tiwanaku people and other ancient residents of the area used the dry soil in the Atacama Desert as a giant scratch pad. More than five thousand geoglyphs have been identified there. These are designs and symbols carved into the ground. People drew the lines and patterns between A.D. 600 and 1500. These ancient artists made lines by scraping away the dark soil on the surface. Their designs appeared in the light-colored soil below the dark layer. They created drawings of people, llamas, monkeys, hummingbirds *(below)* lizards, fish, eagles, and other animals. Some of the drawings are circles, arrows, lines, rectangles, and other geometric figures. Scientists do not know why people drew these patterns or what they mean. The largest one is the outline of a person, called the Atacama Giant. This giant is almost 393 feet (120 m) long.

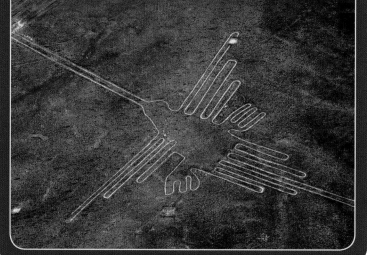

LIFE IN THE DESERT

The word *desert* comes from the Latin word *desertum*. It means "an unpopulated place." Because of the dry, harsh conditions, few plants or animals can survive in deserts. Cactus plants and other desert plants have special adaptations for life in the desert. Their waxy skins reflect sunlight instead of absorbing it. And the skins hold in water, which helps plants survive the dry heat. More than one hundred different kinds of cactus grow in the Atacama.

Desert animals also have adapted to the harsh conditions in the Atacama. Kangaroo rats, for instance, usually hide in burrows during the hottest part of the day. When they are outside, their light coats reflect sunlight.

Amazingly, however, more than one million people live in the Atacama Desert. They have become used to the dry air. (That dry air makes visitors uncomfortable by chapping the lips, cracking the skin, and causing nosebleeds.)

Most of these people live in cities and fishing villages along the coast of the Pacific Ocean. Some work in mines that produce copper, gold, and other metals. Farmers in the far north use water from deep wells. They grow tomatoes, olives, and other crops. In other parts of the desert, descendants of the Atacama people raise llamas and alpacas. These animals are in the camel family. They can thrive in dry conditions.

A DESERT FOR SCIENCE

The Atacama Desert may be a difficult place for people to live in. However, it is a wonderful place for astronomers to study the universe with telescopes. The desert has cloudless skies for almost 350 nights each year. As a result, astronomers can work almost every night. In addition, the Atacama has mountains that offer good positions for viewing stars. The telescopes sit above the thickest layer of Earth's atmosphere. At lower altitudes, that layer of the atmosphere blurs light from incoming stars.

FOG *Catchers*

People in parts of the Atacama Desert buy water that is shipped in on trucks. That water is expensive, so people don't bathe or take showers every day. In some towns and villages, residents have found a source of free water. They catch water from the fog that frequently rolls in off the mountains. The fog-catching equipment consist of fine nets and gutters *(below)*. The gutters resemble the rain gutters that run along the roofs of houses. The nets hang vertically above the gutters. Fog collects on the nets and turns into water, just like dew on the grass on summer mornings. The water drips into the gutters. Pipes carry the water to villages. Fog catchers collect a surprising amount of water. In some villages, they provide about 2,600 gallons (9,841 liters) of water every day.

Above: *The city of Arica, Chile, sits on the Pacific coast, surrounded by the Atacama Desert.*
Below: *The Lluta River, near Arica, makes portions of the Atacama Desert habitable.*

Above: *Visitors to the
Chuquicamata copper
mine can see Peru's
enormous mining
industry in action in the
Atacama.* Left: *These
three large telescopes
are part of the Very
Large Telescope (VLT)
in the Atacama Desert.
The European Southern
Observatory runs the
operations here.*

EVER
Wonder?

Why are there rich mineral resources in the Atacama Desert? The Atacama's extreme dryness has left the soil with rich deposits of minerals, such as sodium nitrate and copper. These deposits exist because rain never washes them away. People have been mining copper in the Atacama since the 1700s.

Sodium nitrate is an ingredient in fertilizers, which farmers use to grow crops. It is also used to make explosives. People began digging for sodium nitrate in the mid-1800s. Eventually about two hundred nitrate mines dotted the desert landscape. During World War I (1914–1918), the mines produced millions of tons of nitrate for bombs and other weapons. The mines closed later in the twentieth century, after scientists discovered a way to make sodium nitrate.

Since the 1960s, astronomers from around the world have been taking advantage of these spectacular conditions. They have built observatories with powerful telescopes for studying distant stars, galaxies, and other objects in outer space. About twenty major observatories are located in the desert. Here astronomers work with some of the world's largest telescopes.

The Atacama Desert also attracts scientists from the National Aeronautics and Space Administration (NASA) in the United States. NASA has used this desolate place to test unmanned space vehicles. NASA wants to use the vehicles to search for life on other planets. In 2005 NASA scientists completed tests of a robotic rover named Zoë in the Atacama Desert. Those scientists did not expect to find any life in the heart of the Atacama. However, they found traces of bacteria growing in cracks in some rocks.

"The Atacama is the only place on the Earth [from which] I've taken soil samples to grow microorganisms back at the lab and nothing whatsoever grew."
— Fred A. Rainey, a scientist at Louisiana State University who studied life in the desert

4 Galápagos Islands

A sea lion sits in a forest of prickly pear cactuses on one of the Galápagos Islands.

$\mathcal{T}$HE GALÁPAGOS ISLANDS ARE HOME
TO STRANGE AND WONDERFUL ANIMALS. MANY OF THESE CREATURES
LIVE NOWHERE ELSE ON EARTH. OTHERS BEHAVE IN WAYS THAT ARE
QUITE UNUSUAL FOR WILD ANIMALS. GIANT TORTOISES WADDLE OVER
THE GROUND, CHOMPING MOUTHFULS OF GRASS AND FLOWERS. SOME
OF THESE LAND TURTLES WEIGH 500 POUNDS (227 KG) AND HAVE
SHELLS 4 FEET (1.2 M) LONG. THEY OFTEN LIVE FOR 150 YEARS.

Land iguanas on the Galápagos look like mini-dragons from a science-fiction story. These lizards have clawed feet and long tails. They can reach lengths of 5 feet (1.5 m) and weigh up to 25 pounds (11 kg).

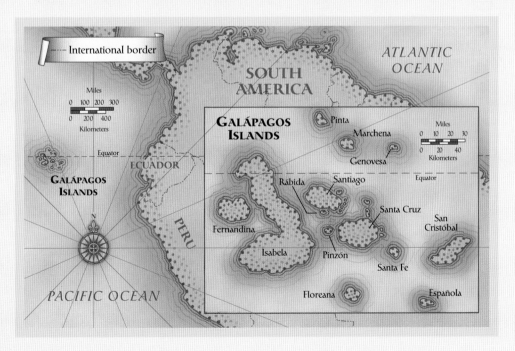

It's hard to miss the bright-colored feet on this pair of blue-footed boobies. The word *booby* comes from the Spanish word *bobo*, or "dunce."

When a visitor sits on a rock near the seashore to enjoy the view, a huge sea lion may hop out of the water. Like many other Galápagos animals, these seal-like creatures act more like pets than wild animals. Instead of fearing people, that sea lion may flop right up to the visitor's feet. Then it may lie down for a nap in the warm sun.

One Galápagos Island bird looks quite ordinary at first glance. It has a white chest and throat with dark brown wings. But those *feet.* They are baby blue in color. That's how this bird got its name, the blue-footed booby. When a male bird wants to impress a female, he stands on one foot and waves the other at her.

These islands were named for one of their wonderful animals. A Spanish bishop, Tomás de Berlanga, discovered the islands in 1535. He was amazed at the tortoises. So de Berlanga named the islands for the tortoises. *Galápago* is the Spanish word for "tortoise."

"We sighted an island . . . [where the sailors] found nothing but seals, turtles and such big tortoises that each could carry a man on top of [itself] and many iguanas that are like serpents."

—*Tomás de Berlanga, a Spanish priest who visited the Galápagos Islands in 1535*

The Galápagos are a chain of thirteen large islands and many small ones in the Pacific Ocean. The islands lie along the equator about 600 miles (966 km) west of Ecuador. The islands are actually a province (district) of Ecuador. The islands have level shorelines with trees and shrubs. Farther inland, the land is desertlike, with cactuses and thorny bushes. Mountains carpeted with lush vegetation rise up near the center of the islands. Some of those mountains are volcanoes that still erupt.

This photograph was taken from an airplane as it flew over Isabela Island in the Galápagos. Isabela is the largest of the Galápagos Islands and is made of six volcanoes. Five of Isabela's volcanoes are still active.

Charles Darwin (right) *sailed on the HMS* Beagle (above) *to the Galápagos Islands in the 1830s. Darwin made many discoveries there that led to his theory of evolution.*

A FAMOUS VISIT

Sailors once were the only people who knew about the Galápagos Islands. On long voyages across the Pacific Ocean, they stopped at the islands to get fresh food and water. One voyage in the 1800s, however, made the Galápagos world famous.

The HMS *Beagle* sailed from Great Britain in 1831 on a scientific expedition. Charles Darwin went aboard as the ship's scientist. Darwin was unknown then. But his observations during the *Beagle*'s five-year journey made him one of the most famous scientists in the world.

At the time, many people shared a belief about the natural world. They thought that all plants and animals on Earth had been created at the same time, as described in the Bible. They thought these plants and animals had changed very little since then. Darwin saw animals on the Galápagos Islands in 1835 that made him question this popular belief.

The Galápagos Islands were named after the huge tortoises sailors found there. People from around the world still travel to the Galápagos to see the giant tortoises as well as the other unusual creatures that live there.

After visiting the coast of South America, the *Beagle* stopped at the Galápagos Islands. The crew wanted fresh supplies of water and food before continuing their journey. In those days, ships often stopped at the Galápagos Islands to collect giant tortoises. Sailors cooked and ate the tortoise meat for food. The islands were famous for the thousands of these big turtles that roamed the land.

The *Beagle*'s crew spent about five weeks collecting tortoises. Darwin used that time to study plant and animal life on the islands. He had done the same thing at other places during the *Beagle*'s expedition. Darwin had already observed the wildlife on the nearby South American coast.

"The [Galápagos] is a little world within itself. . . . Considering the small size of these islands, we feel the more astonished at the number of their aboriginal beings. . . . [I]n both space and time, we seem to be brought somewhat nearer to that great fact—that mystery of mysteries—the first appearance of new beings on this earth."

—*Charles Darwin*, Voyage of the Beagle, *1890*

VAMPIRE BIRDS

On the Galápagos Islands, Darwin found species of plants, reptiles, and birds that looked different from those on the coast. On one dry, desertlike island, the South American green iguana ate sharp-spined cactus plants. On another island, that same type of iguana lived in the sea. Its shorter jaw allowed it to scrape algae off rocks. Its flat tail helped it swim.

The Galápagos's small sparrowlike finches fascinated Darwin. He noticed that similar finches had different types of beaks. Each one worked perfectly for the type of food available in the bird's environment. One species of finch used its broad beak to crack hard cactus seeds. Another reached into cactus blossoms with its curved beak. Still another finch had a sharp beak that was perfect for pecking at seabirds and feeding on their blood! It became known years later as a vampire finch.

After Darwin returned home to Great Britain in 1836, he learned more about the plants on the islands. Darwin had collected

Darwin's drawing of four different species of finches with distinctively shaped heads and beaks

A marine iguana swims off the coast of Fernandina Island.

TORMENTED *Tortoises*

Scientists think that about 250,000 tortoises once lived on the Galápagos Islands. For hundreds of years, sailors stopped at the islands to catch giant tortoises for food. Tortoises were popular with sailors because these animals could be kept alive on ships for up to a year with no food or water. Few people were concerned with how those poor animals might feel. Tortoises gave sailors a supply of fresh meat. Sailors captured so many, however, that some species of tortoise became extinct. Only about fifteen thousand giant tortoises remain on the Galápagos Islands.

hundreds of plants from the islands. He had labeled each one with the name of the island where he found it. Darwin gave the plants to a botanist, a scientist who studies plants. The botanist came to a surprising conclusion. Most plants on each island were different from those on the neighboring islands.

Darwin looked over his notes. And he began asking questions. Why did the animals and plants on each island of the Galápagos seem to change along with their environment?

In 1859 Darwin published a book, *On the Origin of Species.* In it Darwin explained his startling conclusions. He had decided that living things did, indeed, change over long periods of time. They changed to adapt to their environment.

Darwin concluded that animals and plants evolved, or changed gradually, into new species. He believed this was true of living things everywhere and not just in South America. Modern elephants, for instance, do not look the same as elephants that lived in the past. Their ancestors were mammoths with long, curved tusks and coats of wooly hair. Wooly mammoths gradually evolved into modern elephants.

Darwin's idea became known as the theory of evolution. This idea amazed, shocked, and even angered many people around the world. They did not believe that the ancestors of modern human beings could be apes and monkeys.

The theory of evolution changed the study of biology. Until Darwin's visit to the Galápagos Islands, biology was not a modern science. The people who studied biology were naturalists like Darwin. They collected notes on the appearance and habits of living things. Darwin's theory of evolution helped biologists understand the origins of the plants and animals they studied. The Galápagos Islands were crucial to Darwin's theory of evolution.

THE GALÁPAGOS IN THE TWENTY-FIRST CENTURY

Many of the same plants and animals that inspired Charles Darwin still thrive on the Galápagos Islands. The government of Ecuador has made the islands a national park. Rangers in Galápagos National Park make sure that visitors do not harm the plants or animals. More than fifty thousand people visit each year. A scientific research center on the islands, named for Charles Darwin, helps preserve the wildlife. For example, scientists at the station want to increase the number of giant tortoises that live on the islands. They raise baby tortoises that just hatched from their eggs. Scientists release them into the wild.

In 1978 the United Nations Educational, Scientific, and Cultural Organization put the Galápagos on its list of World Heritage Sites. UNESCO wanted the rest of the world to recognize the islands' importance. In 2007, however, the organization expressed concern that increased tourism is harming the islands.

Above: *During the mating season, males compete with each other for female attention by facing each other with open mouths, standing tall, and stretching their heads high.* Below: *Tourists visit Baltra Island, north of Santa Cruz Island.*

5 Montecristo CLOUD FOREST

Specialized plants live in tropical cloud forests, such as this one, called Montecristo Cloud Forest, in Central America.

$\mathcal{I}$N CENTRAL AMERICA, THERE IS A JUNGLE CALLED THE MONTECRISTO CLOUD FOREST. IT SPRAWLS ACROSS A LARGE MOUNTAINOUS AREA OF 4,800 ACRES (1,942 HECTARES). THE FOREST IS WHERE THE BORDERS OF GUATEMALA, HONDURAS, AND EL SALVADOR MEET.

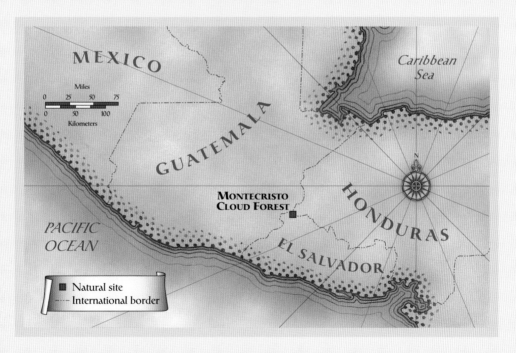

The striped fulvous owl lives in the cloud forests of Central America, such as the Montecristo Cloud Forest.

People sometimes call Montecristo an enchanted forest. It reminds them of forests in fairy tales. No one actually expects to encounter elves or talking animals, of course. But it is a magical place. The trees, shrubs, ferns, and other plants in this forest soak up water from the air.

The Montecristo Cloud Forest is like the enchanted forests of fairy tales in another way. It is filled with plants and animals of almost magical beauty. Soft green mosses, lacy ferns, beautiful orchids, and mushrooms cover the forest floor like a carpet. Some trees have trunks and branches with a gnarled, knotted appearance. They look spooky. Living in the forest are rare spider monkeys, two-fingered anteaters, agoutis (a kind of rodent), pumas, toucans, and striped owls.

EVER *Wonder?*

What is the difference between a cloud forest and a rain forest? Cloud forests differ from rain forests in several ways. Since cloud forests are at higher altitudes, they are much cooler than hot tropical rain forests. Although both types of forest get plenty of rainfall, most of the moisture in cloud forests comes from clouds and mist. They constantly swirl through the trees, hills, and valleys of the forest.

The clouds and mist block much of the direct sunlight. That's why trees in a cloud forest tend to be shorter than those in rain forests. Trees need light to grow. In a cloud forest, tree trunks are thicker and their branches take on a twisted, knotted look.

Clouds and mist blanket the treetops of cloud forests. Moisture from the air provides water for plants and animals living in these tropical habitats and for the local people as well.

A FOREST IN THE CLOUDS

Montecristo is one of a series of cloud forests that stretch from Guatemala in Central America into South America. These forests are in mountainous areas with tropical climates, which are warm and rainy. The forests are constantly covered by clouds and mist. The Montecristo Cloud Forest is certainly high enough to be in the clouds. A large part of it is at an altitude of 7,000 feet (2,134 m). Cloud forests exist in other parts of the world too, including Africa and Asia.

The Montecristo Cloud Forest is west of the Caribbean Sea. Wet tropical trade winds blow from east to west over the sea and onto the land. These winds blow in one direction for long periods of time. They are called trade winds because hundreds of years ago, traders in sailing ships relied on these winds to help them go faster. These streams of warm, moist air blow all the way to the cloud forest. They are forced upward over the

> *"[Cloud forests] are nature's 'water towers,' providing billions of gallons [liters] of fresh, clean, filtered water. They are home to thousands of . . . people, and storehouses of biodiversity, at least 80 percent of which has not yet been catalogued."*
> —John Roach, National Geographic Society, 2001

steep slopes of Montecristo's highlands and mountains. Warm air holds the moisture as water vapor. The water vapor is an invisible gas. As the warm air rises and cools, the water vapor changes into visible droplets. Those droplets of water become the mist, fog, and clouds that blanket the Montecristo Cloud Forest.

WATER NETS

Many of the plants in the Montecristo Cloud Forest are epiphytes, or air plants. They include mosses, ferns, vines, and orchids. These plants look as if they live on air alone. They grow without any connection to the soil. Some epiphytes drape themselves over tree branches and vines. Others grow right on top of other plants.

Epiphytes get their water from the misty air. In fact, they act like water nets. Water droplets in the air collect on those plants. The droplets are like the dew on a lawn on a summer morning. In the Montecristo Cloud Forest, water from the air also collects on tree leaves and drips to the ground.

A single drop does not contain much water. It takes about seventy-six thousand drops from an eyedropper to fill a 1-gallon (3.8-liter) milk jug. But imagine the number of drops that collect on trillions of leaves, ferns, and other plants in the Montecristo Cloud Forest.

OLD MAN'S *Beard*

One water-catching plant in the Montecristo Cloud Forest has an interesting name. It is called Old Man's Beard. This plant has threadlike strands that look like hairs on a beard. It grows over the branches of trees and hangs down like a huge, living net. The hairy strands capture water from the moist air.

Above: *A worker at the Montecristo Cloud Forest checks bromeliads (a type of tropical American epiphyte) at a botanical garden called the Garden of 100 Years. The close-up on the right shows another type of bromeliad. You can tell that it is an epiphyte, because it is growing on the tree rather than in soil.*

"The cloud forest [in Central America] will all be gone in the next ten years."

—*Peruvian biologist Percy Nuñez, 2001*

The water dripping off the trees and plants increases the amount of rain in the Montecristo by 15 to 20 percent.

Most of this clean water goes below the surface of the soil. The water collects there as groundwater. That underground water feeds springs and wells. The wells provide water for people nearby. The Montecristo Cloud Forest is a valuable source of water for local people.

PRESERVING THE CLOUD FOREST

The Montecristo Cloud Forest is a rare wonder. Cloud forests make up only 2.5 percent of the total area of the world's tropical forests. In Central and South America, they account for only 1.2 percent of all tropical forests. Cloud forests face many threats, and scientists are concerned that many of these natural wonders could disappear by 2015.

Deforestation is the main threat to the Montecristo Cloud Forest. People who live near the forest cut down some of the trees for fuel. They burn the wood to cook their food and warm their homes.

The governments of El Salvador, Guatemala, and Honduras have been working together to preserve the Montecristo Cloud Forest. They encourage local people to use stoves that are energy efficient and burn less wood. A conservation program also plans to plant trees that local residents can use for fuel.

A quetzal is a rare bird that makes its home in Central American cloud forests. This one is perched on a branch covered in mosses, ferns, and other epiphytes. Humans must work to preserve this ecosystem if species such as these are to survive.

Poás VOLCANO

Blue sky reflects in the lake water that has collected at the bottom of the Poás volcano crater. The crater is still active. When an erruption happens, hot lava causes jets of water to shoot into the air.

COSTA RICA IS A LAND OF VOLCANOES. EXPERTS HAVE IDENTIFIED ABOUT TWO HUNDRED VOLCANIC FORMATIONS IN COSTA RICA. MOST ARE DORMANT. THEY NO LONGER ERUPT. ONE OF THE MOST ACTIVE VOLCANOES IS POÁS. POÁS IS THE ONLY VOLCANO ON EARTH WHERE SCIENTISTS HAVE FOUND SULFUR LAKES.

Poás rises nearly 8,900 feet (2,713 m) above sea level. It is about 29 miles (47 km) from San José, the capital of Costa Rica. Like many other volcanoes, Poás blows red-hot lava out of holes, which are called vents.

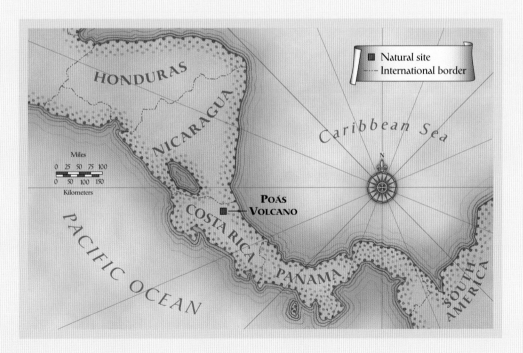

Above: *Steam rises and water boils in Poás volcano's main crater.* Below: *The volcano's extinct Botos crater has filled with water to make Lake Botos, a lush lake surrounded by tropical trees and flowers. A third crater (not pictured), called Von Frantzius, is also extinct.*

Why does a volcano erupt? Earth is very hot at its center. As this heat rises, it melts some of the rock in Earth's interior. The molten (melted) rock looks like red-hot toothpaste. Molten rock is lighter than the surrounding rock. So it rises toward the surface. Often, the molten rock gradually cools. Sometimes, though, it keeps pushing toward the surface. As the molten rock rises, it fills with gases. The gas bubbles force the molten rock through cracks in the surface of Earth. Once molten rock is forced out of the volcano, it is called lava *(below)*. The lava bursts out of the volcano along with ash and gases.

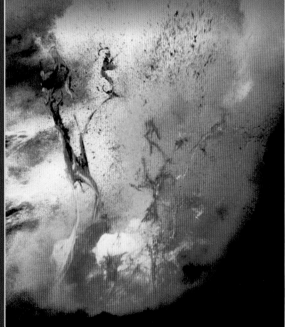

AMAZING SULFUR LAKES

Poás has a very large active crater, which measures almost 1 mile (1.6 km) across. The crater is 900 feet (274 m) deep. It is one of the largest craters in any volcano in the world.

Rainwater collects in the bottom of this huge hole and has formed a small lake. It is called Laguna Caliente, which is Spanish for "hot lake." When hot lava touches the water in the bottom of the lake, it sets off a reaction. The water boils and creates steam. Huge jets of steam and hot water shoot into the air. These jets are called geysers. Some geysers on Poás rise 328 feet (100 m) into the air.

In 1989 scientists found lakes of liquid sulfur under Laguna Caliente. Sulfur is normally a pale yellow powdery material. When it's heated, however, it becomes a liquid. This liquid has the unforgettable smell of rotten eggs. Much of Earth's sulfur lies underground.

Scientists had long believed that lakes of liquid sulfur existed on Earth. They thought these lakes lay at the bottoms of craters in active volcanoes. In 1989 Laguna Caliente dried up for a few months. With the water gone, scientists examined the crater floor. They saw liquid sulfur lakes. It was the first time anyone had observed a sulfur lake on Earth.

Some scientists believe that when the water in the crater evaporated, the floor of the crater became much hotter. As a result, sulfur at the bottom of the crater turned to liquid.

Experts have seen sulfur lakes in only one other place. They have seen them on Io in outer space. Io is one of the moons circling the giant planet Jupiter. The unmanned spacecraft *Voyager 1* first detected signs of sulfur lakes in 1979. It radioed images of them back to scientists on Earth.

Poás has another crater lake called Lake Botos. It does not contain liquid sulfur but sits in the middle of a cloud forest.

THE SMELL OF TROUBLE

Scientists worry that Poás may threaten Costa Rica's environment. Laguna Caliente eventually refilled with water. Sulfur gases constantly bubble up into the water. When sulfur mixes with water, it forms an acid. The acid is strong enough to burn skin and eat through metal. Laguna Caliente has become the most acidic lake in the world. Its acid water seeps underground. Scientists worry that the acid water may travel far. It could spoil the water in streams and in wells. People use this water for drinking, bathing, and watering crops.

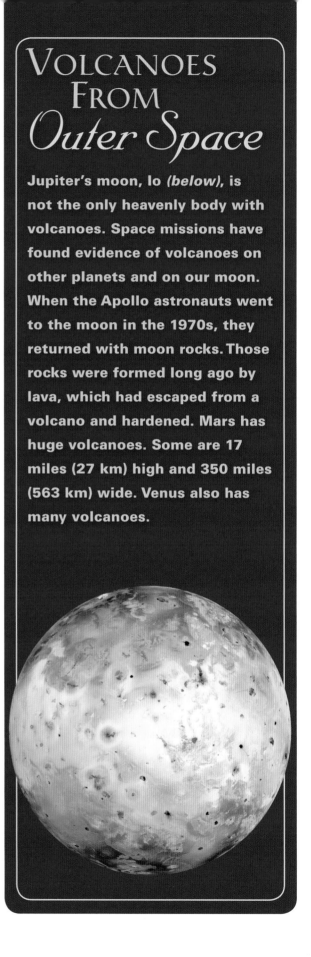

VOLCANOES FROM *Outer Space*

Jupiter's moon, Io *(below)*, is not the only heavenly body with volcanoes. Space missions have found evidence of volcanoes on other planets and on our moon. When the Apollo astronauts went to the moon in the 1970s, they returned with moon rocks. Those rocks were formed long ago by lava, which had escaped from a volcano and hardened. Mars has huge volcanoes. Some are 17 miles (27 km) high and 350 miles (563 km) wide. Venus also has many volcanoes.

A hiker stops to admire the forest along a trail in Poás Volcano National Park.

Laguna Caliente releases acidic sulfur gases from the crater. The poisonous gas turns nearby vegetation brown. The yellow color in the crater is a result of the sulfur, which is commonly found at hot springs and volcanic areas around the world.

> *"One look at the volcano, and it is easy to believe that Poás still has plenty of energy bottled up inside it. One could see bubbles on the lava's surface and smoke above the crater . . . the volcano exploded 15 years ago."*
>
> —*Simluck Srimalee, a reporter who visited Poás in 2005*

VOLCANOES in Paradise

Costa Rica has many volcanoes because of its location. Earth's outer crust is made from enormous plates of rock. The plates move slowly, and their edges bump and grind against one another. Costa Rica sits above a place where two plates collide. One plate sometimes pushes the other down below the surface of Earth. The rock in this plate comes close to the hot interior of Earth and melts. The melted rock begins to rise toward Earth's crust.

Costa Rica's volcanoes have helped create a tropical paradise. Ash from volcanic eruptions is rich in nutrients. The nutrients fertilize plants in the tropical rain forests.

Some of the sulfur in Laguna Caliente escapes as gas instead of mixing with the water. The wind spreads the gases around. When it rains, the gases form acid rain. Acid rain damages tropical rain forest plants. It may harm animals living in the forest too.

POÁS VOLCANO NATIONAL PARK

Poás is part of a national park in Costa Rica called Poás Volcano National Park. Many farms and thousands of homes lie inside the park's boundaries. The park also includes a cloud forest with many beautiful plants, birds, and other animals. Those attractions draw two hundred thousand visitors to the park each year. When the volcano is quiet, people can walk close to the edge of its crater and look inside. Rangers often must close the park, however, when it threatens to erupt. Poás first erupted in 1828 and has erupted forty times since then.

7 Andes MOUNTAINS

Seen from above, the Andes Mountain range looks like giant ripples in the land.

*H*UMANS HAVE A BACKBONE OR SPINE. THIS COLUMN OF THIRTY-THREE BONES RUNS ALONG THE BACK, FROM TOP TO BOTTOM. THE TOPS OF THOSE BONES FEEL LIKE BUMPS RUNNING ALONG THE CENTER OF THE BACK.

The continent of South America also has a kind of backbone. Thousands of mountains stretch along the length of the continent from its top to its bottom. They cover a distance of more than 5,000 miles (8,000 km). This mountain range is called the Andes Mountains. It is the longest mountain range in the world.

The Andes lie along the western edge of South America. They rise up from the Pacific Ocean and extend inland in a narrow ridge. The mountain range usually is about 200 miles (322 km) wide. It reaches into seven countries: Venezuela, Colombia, Ecuador, Peru, Bolivia, Chile, and Argentina.

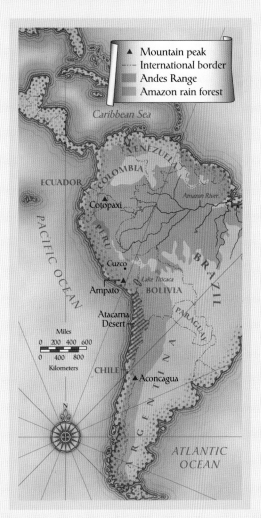

- ▲ Mountain peak
- --- International border
- Andes Range
- Amazon rain forest

The snowcapped peak of Aconcagua, the highest mountain in the Andes, rises in the distance.

The Andes include some of the world's highest mountains. More than forty mountains in the Andes range soar higher than 20,000 feet (6,100 m) above sea level. One of them is Aconcagua in Argentina, near the border of Chile. Aconcagua is 22,841 feet (6,962 m) high. It is the highest mountain in the Western Hemisphere and Southern Hemisphere. Only the Himalaya mountains are higher than the Andes. That range of mountains in central Asia includes Mount Everest, the world's highest mountain. It is 29,035 feet (8,850 m) above sea level.

THE BEGINNING OF THE "BACKBONE"

The Andes formed more than 130 million years ago. At that time, the continents of Earth were still forming. Originally there was only one C-shaped continent, which lay along the equator. This gigantic landmass was called Pangaea. Underneath Pangaea were giant plates of rock. Pangaea began to break apart about 200 million years ago, when the giant plates of rock drifted away from one another. As Pangaea broke apart, its pieces formed seven continents.

While the continents were still separating, major mountains formed. They formed in areas where two plates collided. One plate moved under the other, pushing it up. Think of a snow shovel under a sheet of ice on a sidewalk or driveway. The Andes began forming when the plate of rock covered by the Pacific Ocean slowly slid beneath the South American plate. Those two plates continue to grind against each other. They cause earthquakes and volcanic eruptions in the Andes.

THE RAINMAKER

Most of the highest mountains in the Andes are volcanoes. They formed when hot lava, gas, and ash poured out of openings in Earth's surface. Many of the Andes' volcanoes are dormant, but some are active. These include Cotopaxi in Ecuador. Cotopaxi soars 19,347 feet (5,897 m) above sea level. It is the highest active volcano in the world.

The Andes have influenced the environment of the entire continent of South America. They have helped produce the largest rain forest on Earth, the

Ecuador's Cotopaxi pokes its head through the clouds.

The Andes form a majestic backdrop behind the deep blue waters of Lake Titicaca.

Amazon rain forest. The forest is east of the Andes Mountains. The mountains block the air masses that move across South America. When moist air from the Atlantic Ocean reaches the Andes, it must rise to pass over the high peaks. As the air rises and cools, it releases its moisture as rain. That rain falls on land to the east of the Andes, soaking the rain forest.

Rain and snow also fall on the eastern slopes. This precipitation feeds mountain streams in the Andes. They are the source, or starting point, of the great river systems of South America. The rivers include the Amazon, the world's second-longest river, which flows through Peru and Brazil.

The Andes also increase precipitation (rain and snow) over large mountain lakes. One is the enormous Lake Titicaca, on the border between Peru and Bolivia. Lake Titicaca sits on a high plateau in the Andes Mountains at an elevation of 12,500 feet (3,800 m). It covers an area of 3,200 square miles (8,288 sq. km).

The Andes have also helped create an extremely dry land. The Atacama Desert stretches in a narrow band to the west of the Andes, along the Pacific coast.

EVER *Wonder?*

Are there glaciers, or ice sheets, in South America? The Quelccaya Ice Cap *(below)* in the Andes Mountains is the largest glacier in any tropical area of the world. This enormous ice sheet in southern Peru covers an area of about 17 square miles (44 sq. km). In some spots, it is about 500 feet (153 m) thick. The ice stays frozen because the glacier is high in the mountains, where temperatures are cold year-round.

THE INCA OF THE ANDES

Rock that pushed up to form the Andes was rich in minerals. As a result, these mountains hold large deposits of gold, silver, copper, platinum, mercury, lead, and iron.

Some of that gold and silver enriched the great Inca Empire. In the 1400s, this empire stretched for 2,400 miles (3,862 km) from what is modern Ecuador to central Chile. The Inca people made Cuzco the capital of their empire. The city lies in southern Peru, in a valley of the Andes Mountains.

Visitors to modern Cuzco can see the remains of Inca stone walls and a temple. The Inca were exceptional builders. They

The Quelccaya Ice Cap in Peru lies at about 18,600 feet (5,470 m) above sea level in the Andes.

cut stone blocks so that the edges were straight and the blocks fit together perfectly. With these blocks, they built houses, temples, fountains, and staircases.

The Inca were also good engineers. They carved terraces out of the steep slopes of the Andes Mountains. These terraces looked like steps covered with soil. They gave farmers flat surfaces for growing crops.

When the Spanish conquered the Inca in the 1500s, they destroyed many of their fine buildings. But the Spanish overlooked the city of Machu Picchu, northwest of Cuzco. The Inca had built this small city on a ridge between two mountains. A U.S. explorer named Hiram Bingham visited Machu Picchu in 1911. The Inca's graceful temples, long staircases, and carefully built houses amazed Bingham. Bingham wrote magazine stories and books that made Machu Picchu famous around the world.

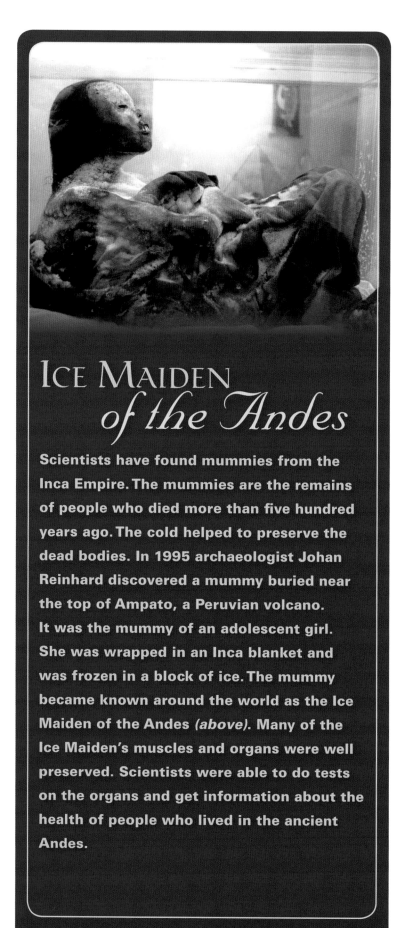

ICE MAIDEN
of the Andes

Scientists have found mummies from the Inca Empire. The mummies are the remains of people who died more than five hundred years ago. The cold helped to preserve the dead bodies. In 1995 archaeologist Johan Reinhard discovered a mummy buried near the top of Ampato, a Peruvian volcano. It was the mummy of an adolescent girl. She was wrapped in an Inca blanket and was frozen in a block of ice. The mummy became known around the world as the Ice Maiden of the Andes (above). Many of the Ice Maiden's muscles and organs were well preserved. Scientists were able to do tests on the organs and get information about the health of people who lived in the ancient Andes.

"In the variety of its charms and the power of its spell, I know of no place in the world which can compare with it . . . great snow peaks looming above the clouds more than two miles [3 km] overhead; gigantic precipices of many-colored granite rising sheer for thousands of feet above the foaming, glistening, roaring rapids."

— U.S. explorer Hiram Bingham, describing
a canyon carved by the Urubamba River
in the Peruvian Andes, 1922

In 1911 U.S. explorer Hiram Bingham came across Machu Picchu (above) high in the Andes Mountains. He called it the Lost City of the Incas.

Using techniques developed by their ancestors, Peruvians have carved terraces in the steep mountainsides to grow crops.

PEOPLE OF THE ANDES

Modern visitors to Machu Picchu and other places in the Andes sometimes feel uncomfortable. The air contains less oxygen at high altitudes. People who are not used to these altitudes have more trouble breathing, and they become exhausted easily.

Local people have adjusted to life in low-oxygen conditions. Miners in Chile and Peru, for instance, dig minerals out of the ground in some of the world's highest mines. Many of those mines are at elevations of more than 15,000 feet (4,572 m).

Farmers in mountainous areas live and work in much the same way as their Inca ancestors did. Farmers plant crops on hillside terraces because flatland with good soil is scarce. They grow potatoes and grain. Farmers also raise llamas and alpacas. These camel-like animals thrive at high altitudes. Llamas are used as pack animals to carry people and goods. They also provide wool, milk, and meat. Alpacas are smaller animals that provide a very soft and fine kind of wool.

Herds of sheep and alpaca graze on the slopes of the Andes in Santa Rosa, Peru.

TIMELINE

600–1500	Geoglyphs appear in the Atacama Desert.
1535	A Spanish bishop, Tomás de Berlanga, discovers the islands of Galápagos and names them after the tortoises he saw there.
1541	Francisco de Orellana travels the entire length of the Amazon River.
1831	The HMS *Beagle* sets sail from Great Britain on a scientific expedition with Charles Darwin on board as the ship's scientist.
1859	Charles Darwin publishes *On the Origin of Species,* his theory of evolution, based on his findings on the Galápagos Islands.
1911	Hiram Bingham re-discovers Machu Picchu and calls it the Lost City of the Incas.
1935	The U.S. pilot Jimmy Angel discovers Angel Falls in Venezuela.
1949	The U.S. journalist Ruth Robertson measures the height of Angel Falls and finds that it is the world's highest waterfall.
1989	Laguna Caliente, the lake in the big crater of Poás volcano, dries up. Scientists can see molten sulfur lakes on the crater floor.
1990s	Loggers clear about 7,700 square miles (19,943 sq. km) of the Amazon rain forest each year.
1994	UNESCO names Canaima National Park in Venezuela to the list of World Heritage Sites.
1995	Archaeologist Johan Reinhard discovers a mummy, known as the Ice Maiden, in the Peruvian Andes.
2005	NASA scientists are surprised to discover life in the middle of the Atacama Desert. They find traces of bacteria growing in cracks in some rocks.
2007	Brazilian scientists confirm the source of the Amazon River is on the slope of a mountain in southern Peru called Nevado Mismi. They report the river is 4,225 miles (6,800 km) long and is therefore the world's longest river.
2008	Oil companies search for oil and gas in previously untouched areas of the Amazon rain forest.

CHOOSE AN EIGHTH WONDER

Now that you've read about the seven natural wonders of Central and South America, do a little research to choose an eighth wonder. You may enjoy working with a friend.

To do your research, look at some of the websites and books listed on pages 76 and 77. Look for places in Central and South America that

- *are especially large*
- *are exceptionally beautiful*
- *were unknown to foreigners for many centuries*
- *are unlike any other place on Earth*

You might even try gathering photos and writing your own chapter on the eighth wonder!

GLOSSARY AND PRONUNCIATION GUIDE

Atacama (AH-tah-KAH-mah): a desert in northern Chile with the driest desert land on Earth

Auyantepui (eye-ahn-tay-POO-ee): the flat-topped mountain in Venezuela from which Angel Falls spills down

cloud forest: a forest in a mountainous area with a tropical climate that often has low-lying clouds and mist

crust: the outer surface of Earth, which is made from huge plates of rock

desert: dry land that gets less than 10 inches (25 cm) of rain or other precipitation per year

epiphytes: plants that collect water and nutrients from the air and rain rather than the soil

erosion: wearing away of rock and soil by wind, rain, or rivers

evolution: the theory that living things gradually change to adapt to their environment

Galápagos (guh-LAH-puh-gohs): islands off the coast of Ecuador with very unusual wildlife

molten rock: rock that has been changed into a liquid by heat

Montecristo (mawn-tay-KRIHS-toh): a large cloud forest in Central America

mouth: the place where a river ends, usually by flowing into an ocean or lake

Nevado Mismi (nay-VAH-doh MIHZ-mee): a mountain in southern Peru that scientists believe is the location of the source of the Amazon River

Pemón (pay-MOHN): the local people who live in the region of Venezuela where Angel Falls is located

Poás (poh-AHS): a volcano in Costa Rica with sulfur lakes

rain forest: dense forests that receive at least 80 inches (200 cm) of rain or more a year and are home to many plants and animals. Some rain forests get up to 430 inches (1,090 cm) of rain a year.

source: the place where a river begins to flow

sulfur: a pale yellow mineral that forms acids when mixed with water

tepui (tay-POO-ee): a flat-topped mountain in the country of Venezuela

volcano: an opening in Earth's surface through which melted rock and gases occasionally burst forth

waterfall: water that falls or flows rapidly downward, such as when a river or stream flows from a higher level to a lower level (down a steep descent or over the edge of a cliff, for example)

SOURCE NOTES

8 Sir Walter Raleigh, *The Works of Sir Walter Raleigh, Kt,* vol. 3, eds. William Oldys and Thomas Birch (Oxford, UK: Oxford University Press, 1829), 455.

9 James Angel, quoted in Tulio R. Soto, "Angel's Horns," *The Lost World,* 2007, http://www.thelostworld.org/laahs/jimmie1.htm (October 1, 2007).

13 Ruth Robertson, "Jungle Journey to the World's Highest Waterfall," *National Geographic,* November 1949, 671.

19 Theodore Roosevelt, *Through the Brazilian Wilderness,* available online at *Alex Catalogue of Electronic Texts,* September 28, 2004, http://infomotions.com/etexts/gutenberg/dirs/1/1/7/4/11746/11746.htm (October 26, 2007).

29 Alonso de Ercilla, quoted in Fernand Braudel, *The Perspective of the World,* vol. 3, *Civilization and Capitalism* (New York: Harper Collins, 1984).

35 Fred A. Rainey, quoted in Rob Anderson, "Mars on Earth?" *EurekAlert,* January 13, 2004, http://www.eurekalert.org/pub_releases/2004-01/lsu-moe011304.php (September 4, 2007).

38 Tomás de Berlanga, "A Letter to His Majesty from Fray Tomás de Berlanga, Describing His Voyage from Panamá to Puerto Viejo, and the Hardships He Encountered in This Navigation," at John Woram, *Las Encatadas: Human and Cartographic History of the Galápagos Islands,* 2007, http://www.galapagos.to/TEXTS/BERLANGA.htm (October 24, 2007).

41 Charles Darwin, *The Voyage of the Beagle: Journal of Researches into the Natural History and Geology of the Countries Visited during the Voyage of the H.M.S. Beagle Round the World* (NewYork: Appleton, 1890), 397.

50 John Roach,"Cloud Forests Fading in the Mist, Their Treasures Little Known," *National Geographic News,* August 13, 2001, http://news.nationalgeographic.com/news/2001/08/0813_cloudforest_2.html (October 23, 2007).

52 Percy Nunez, quoted in John Roach,"Cloud Forests Fading in the Mist, Their Treasures Little Known," *National Geographic News,* August 13, 2001, http://news.nationalgeographic.com/news/2001/08/0813_cloudforest_2.html (October 23, 2007).

61 Simluck Srimalee, "Treasures Among the Trees," *Nation,* October 29, 2005, 8.

69 Hiram Bingham, *Inca Land: Explorations in the Highlands of Peru,* 1922, available online at *Project Gutenberg,* January 21, 2004, http://www.gutenberg.org/files/10772/10772-8.txt (April 24, 2008).

71 UNESCO, "Los Glaciares," *UNESCO World Heritage,* 1982, http://whc.unesco.org/en/list/145 (May 31, 2008).

Selected Bibliography

Allaby, Michael. *Deserts*. New York: Chelsea House, 2006.

Allan, Tony, and Andrew Warren, eds. *Deserts: The Encroaching Wilderness*. New York: Oxford University Press, 1993.

Cleare, John. *Mountains of the World*. San Diego: Thunder Bay, 1997.

Collins, Mark, ed. *The Last Rain Forests: A World Conservation Atlas*. New York: Oxford University Press, 1990.

Darwin, Charles. *The Voyage of the Beagle: Journal of Researches into the Natural History and Geology of the Countries Visited during the Voyage of H.M.S. Beagle Round the World*. New York: Modern Library, 2001.

Flegg, Jim. *Deserts: Miracle of Life*. New York: Facts on File, 1993.

Hancock, Paul, and Brian J. Skinner, eds. *The Oxford Companion to the Earth*. Oxford, UK: Oxford University Press, 2000.

Luhr, James F., ed. *Earth*. London: Dorling Kindersley, 2003.

Stephens, John Lloyd. *Incidents of Travel in Central America, Chiapas, and Yucatan*. 1853. Reprint, Washington, DC: Smithsonian, 1993.

Stewart, Paul D. *Galápagos: The Islands That Changed the World*. New Haven, CT: Yale University Press, 2007.

Veblen, Thomas T., Kenneth R. Young, and Anthony R. Orme, eds. *The Physical Geography of South America*. New York: Oxford University Press, 2007.

Further Reading and Websites

Ibbotson, Eva. *Journey to the River Sea*. New York: Dutton, 2001. Maia, an orphan from London, goes to live with her relatives in Brazil, near the Amazon River. Maia gets involved in an adventure on the Amazon River, where she looks for a lost tribe and a giant sloth.

MacQuitty, Miranda. *Desert*. New York: DK Children, 2000. Find out about some of the most extreme areas of Earth in this Eyewitness title. MacQuitty explains how people live in desert areas around the world.

Moore, Robert J., Jr. *Natural Wonders of the World*. New York: Abbeville, 2000. Moore provides photographs of some of the most beautiful and exotic areas of the world. He explains the various ecosystems and gives an overview of each area's geology and natural history.

Osborne, Mary Pope. *Afternoon on the Amazon*. New York: Random House, 1995. Jack and Annie find themselves traveling back in time to the Amazon rain forest. They try to solve the mystery of the missing magician Morgen le Fay and risk getting eaten by crocodiles and jaguars.

Smith, Miranda, ed. *Jungle*. New York: DK Children, 2004. Great photographs in this Eyewitness book show animals and plants from jungles around the world, including Central America. The book explains the differences between montane (cloud) forests and rain forests.

Streissguth, Tom. *Brazil in Pictures*. Minneapolis: Twenty-First Century Books, 2003. This book describes Brazil's land, history, culture, economy, and more.

Tagliaferro, Linda. *Galápagos Islands: Nature's Delicate Balance at Risk*. Minneapolis: Twenty-First Century Books, 2001. This book in the Discovery! series gives readers information about the fascinating plants and animals that live in this unique ecosystem.

Woods, Michael and Mary B. Woods. *Volcanoes*. Minneapolis: Twenty-First Century Books, 2007. This title in the Disasters Up Close series describes how volcanoes form, the damage they create, and the steps governments are taking to keep their citizens informed about future eruptions. Many of the volcanoes are in Central and South America.

Websites

Galápagos Conservancy

http://www.galapagos.org

You will find all the information you need on the diversity of life on the Galápagos Islands, illustrated with beautiful photographs. The site includes a history of the islands.

Journey into Amazonia

http://www.pbs.org/journeyintoamazonia

Find out about the Amazon rain forest. Click on the link to see the forest flooded with melting snow from the Andes. You can also see pictures of jaguars and learn about life in the treetops of the rain forest.

Mongabay.com

http://kids.mongabay.com

This site is dedicated to educating people about the fragility of rain forests around the world. The site for kids will help you find answers to your questions about the people, plants, and animals that live in the rain forests.

vgsbooks.com

http://www.vgsbooks.com

Visit vgsbooks.com, the homepage of the Visual Geography Series®. You can get linked to all sorts of useful on-line information, including geographical, historical, and cultural websites. The vgsbooks.com site is a great resource for late-breaking news and statistics

What's It Like Where You Live? Biomes of the World

http://www.mbgnet.net

A visit to this site, presented by the Missouri Botanical Gardens, is a great way to learn about the biomes of the world. Just click on the picture, and you will learn interesting facts about deserts, rain forests, forests, grasslands and rivers.

INDEX

kangaroo rats, 31

Laguna Caliente, 58, 60–61
Lake Botos, 56, 58
lakes, sulfur, 55, 58
Lake Titicaca, 67
lava, 57
llamas, 32, 70
logging, 24–25
Lost City of the Incas, 69
Lost World, The, 14
Lluta River, 33

Machu Picchu, 68–69
maps, 7, 17, 27, 37, 47, 55, 63
Mars, 58
McCracken, J. R., 8–9
minerals and mines, 8, 10, 34, 35, 67, 70
molten rock, 57
monkeys, 23, 48
moons, 58
Montecristo Cloud Forest, 46–53; animals of, 48; climate of, 49–50; height of, 49; map of, 47; plants of, 50–52
mountains, 8, 13, 30, 32, 39; flat-topped, 8, 9, 13, 14; world's highest, 64. *See also* Andes Mountains
Mount Everest, 64
mummies, Incan, 68

NASA (National Aeronautics and Space Administration), 35
national parks, 13, 14, 44, 61, 71
Nevado Mismi, 18
Niagara Falls, 8, 12
Nicaragua, 5
Nile River, 18

oil (petroleum), 25
Old Man's Beard, 50
On the Origin of the Species, 43–44
Orellana, Francisco de, 18
otters, 23

Pacific Ocean, 39, 63

Panama, 5
Pangaea, 64
Paraguay, 5
Pemón people, 13
Peru, 5, 17, 26, 63, 67. *See also* Andes Mountains; Atacama Desert
piranha, 22
plants, 13, 21; desert, 31; forest, 24–25, 46, 48, 49, 50–52; Galápagos, 39, 42–43
Poás Volcano, 54–61; crater of, 54, 56; map of, 55; size of, 57; sulfur lakes of, 55, 58–61
Poás Volcano National Park, 59, 61

Quelccaya Ice Cap, 67
quetzal, 53

rain and precipitation, 21, 27, 28, 30, 50, 52
Rainey, Fred A., 35
rain forests, 21–25, 61, 65–66; compared to cloud forests, 48
rain shadow deserts, 30
Raleigh, Walter, 8
Reinhard, Johan, 68
rivers, 8, 19, 21, 28, 33; measuring, 18; sources of, 18; world's longest, 18. *See also* Amazon River
Roach, John, 50
Robertson, Ruth, 11, 13
Roosevelt, Theodore, 19

Sahara, 28
salt basins, 29
sea lions, 36, 38
Seven Wonders of the World, 4–5
sloths, 22
snakes, 23
sodium nitrate, 35
South America, 5, 21; countries of, 5; mountain "backbone" of, 63; population of, 5. *See also* Andes Mountains
space exploration, 35, 58

Srimalee, Simluck, 61
sulfur lakes, 55, 58
Suriname, 5

Tapuyas people, 18
tepuis, 8, 9, 13, 14
Tiwanaku people, 31
tortoises, 37, 38, 41, 43, 45
tourism, 14, 25, 41, 44–45, 61
transportation, 14, 19, 20, 21
tropical climate, 49, 61

UNESCO (United Nations Educational, Scientific and Cultural Organization), 14, 44, 70
Uruguay, 5

vampire birds, 5, 42
Venezuela, 5, 7, 63. *See also* Andes Mountains; Angel Falls
Venus, 58
Very Large Telescope (VLT), 34
volcanoes, 39, 55, 65, 68; eruptions of, 57; highest, 65; on other planets. 58. *See also* Poás Volcano
Voyage of the Beagle, 41
Voyager I, 58

water, 19–20, 21, 33, 50, 52, 58
waterfalls, 5; heights of, 12. *See also* Angel Falls
water vapor, 50
weapons, 35
women, 18
World Heritage Sites, 14, 44
World War I, 35

ABOUT THE AUTHORS

Michael Woods is a science journalist in Washington, D.C., who has won many national writing awards. Mary B. Woods is a librarian in the Fairfax County Public School System in Virginia. Their previous books include the eight-volume Ancient Technology series and the fifteen-volume Disasters Up Close series. The Woodses have four children. When not writing, reading, or enjoying their grandchildren, they travel to gather material for future books.

PHOTO ACKNOWLEDGMENTS

The images in this book are used with the permission of: © age fotostock/SuperStock, pp. 5, 29, 39, 56 (both); © Carl Mydans/Time & Life Pictures/Getty Images, p. 6; © Laura Westlund/Independent Picture Service, pp. 7, 17, 27, 37, 47, 55, 63; © Krzysztof Dydynski/Lonely Planet Images/Getty Images, p. 9; By Gustavo Heny © 2006 Jimmie Angel Historical Project in association with Enrique Lucca Collection, p. 10 (top); © 1996 Jimmie Angel Historical Project, p. 10 (bottom); Harry Ransom Humanities Research Center, The University of Texas at Austin, p. 11; © Bob Masters/Art Directors & TRIP, p. 12; AP Photo/Leslie Mazoch, p. 13; © Prisma/SuperStock, p. 14; © Ken Fisher/Stone/Getty Images, p. 15; © Steve Vidler/SuperStock, p. 16; © David Tomlinson/Alamy, p. 18; © Evaristo Sa/AFP/Getty Images, p. 19; NASA/GSFC/JPL, MISR Team, p. 20; © Medioimages/Photodisc/Getty Images, p. 21 (left); © Gerry Lemmo, pp. 21 (right), 22 (top), 25, 45 (bottom), 51 (bottom), 59; © Paul A. Zahl/ National Geographic/Getty Images, p. 22 (bottom); © Claus Meyer/Minden Pictures/Getty Images, p. 23 (top and bottom right); © Pete Oxford/Minden Pictures/Getty Images, p. 23 (bottom left); AP Photo/Alberto Cesar-Greenpeace/HO, p. 24; © Judy Drew/Art Directors & TRIP, p. 26; © Karlene Schwartz, pp. 28, 70; © Wolfgang Kaehler, 2009-www.wkaehlerphoto.com, p. 30; © Tom Till/Photographer's Choice/Getty Images, p. 31; © Joel Sartore/National Geographic/Getty Images, p. 32; © Martin Barlow/Art Directors & TRIP, pp. 33 (top), 34 (top); © Tui De Roy/Minden Pictures/Getty Images, pp. 33 (bottom), 73 (bottom middle); © Priit Vesilind/National Geographic/Getty Images, p. 34 (bottom); © Jeff Greenberg/Art Directors & TRIP, p. 36; © Kevin Schafer/ The Image Bank/Getty Images, p. 38; © Bettmann/CORBIS, p. 40 (top); © Bridgeman Art Library, London/ SuperStock, p. 40 (bottom); © Mark Jones/Danita Delimont Agency/drr.net, p. 41; © Image Asset Management Ltd./SuperStock, p. 42; © Brian Gadsby/Art Directors & TRIP, p. 43; © Norbert Wu/Science Faction/Getty Images, p. 45 (top); © Knut Eisermann, pp. 46, 48, 53, 73 (top left); © Andrea Alborno/Art Directors & TRIP, pp. 49, 54; © Tomasz Tomaszewski/National Geographic Society Image Collection, p. 51 (top); © Photodisc/Getty Images, p. 57; NASA/JPL, p. 58; © Brian Vikander/Art Directors & TRIP, p. 60; © Kim Steele/The Image Bank/ Getty Images, p. 62; © DEA Picture Library/De Agostini Picture Library/Getty Images, p. 64; © Arctic-Images/ Iconica/Getty Images, p. 65; © Martin Gray/National Geographic/Getty Images, p. 66; © Peter Essick/Aurora/ Getty Images, p. 67; AP Photo/Martin Mejia, p. 68; © Mark Harris/Stone/Getty Images, p. 69; © Warren Jacobs/ Art Directors & TRIP, p. 71; © Travel Ink/Gallo Images/Getty Images, p. 73 (top middle); © Luis Veiga/The Image Bank/Getty Images, p. 73 (top right); © Jeff Rotman/Iconica/Getty Images, p. 73 (left middle); © iStockphoto. com/Birgit Prentner, p. 73 (bottom left); © Colin Monteath/Hedgehog House/Minden Pictures/Getty Images, p. 73 (bottom right).

Front Cover: © Luis Veiga/The Image Bank/Getty Images (top left); © Travel Ink/Gallo Images/Getty Images (top middle); © Knut Eisermann (top right); © Jeff Rotman/Iconica/Getty Images (middle); © iStockphoto.com/ Birgit Prentner (bottom left); © Tui De Roy/Minden Pictures/Getty Images (bottom middle); © Colin Monteath/ Hedgehog House/Minden Pictures/Getty Images (bottom right).